W9-BMU-080

MIND-BLOWING
MAKEUP
IN SPECIAL EFFECTS

BY DANIELLE S. HAMMELEF

Content Consultant:
Mira LaCous
President
Hollywood Pyrotechnics, Inc.

Reading Consultant:
Barbara J. Fox
Professor Emerita
North Carolina State University

CAPSTONE PRESS
a capstone imprint

Blazers Books are published by Capstone Press,
1710 Roe Crest Drive, North Mankato, Minnesota 56003
www.capstonepub.com

Library of Congress Cataloging-in-Publication Data
Hammelef, Danielle S.
Mind-blowing makeup in special effects / by Danielle S Hammelef.
    pages cm
Summary: "Explains how makeup special effects are used in movies"—Provided
by publisher.
Includes bibliographical references and index.
ISBN 978-1-4914-2002-7 (library binding)
ISBN 978-1-4914-2179-6 (eBook PDF)
1. Film makeup—Juvenile literature. I. Title.
PN2068.H225 2015
791.4302′7—dc23   2014028938

Editorial Credits
Brenda Haugen, editor; Aruna Rangarajan, designer; Jo Miller, media researcher;
Tori Abraham, production specialist

Photo Credits
Alamy: Adrian Buck, 15, Catalin Petolea, cover, Moviestore collection Ltd,
29, WENN Ltd, 20, ZUMA Press, Inc., 11; Corbis: Demotix/Malcolm Park, 19;
Photoshot: Xinhua/Luo Xiaoquang, 4; Shutterstock: Couperfield, 16, val lawless,
12; The Kobal Collection: AMC-TV, 25, Cinema Center, 27, Cinemarque-Film
Futures/New World, 21, Gaeta/Rosenzweig Films, 28, Lion's Gate Films/Creep
Entertainment, 8, Mission Control Media, 7, 23

Design Elements
Shutterstock: 21, ARENA Creative, Attitude, Canicula, donatas1205,
escova, freelanceartist, ilolab, Janaka Dharmasena, Matusciac Alexandru,
NikolayPetrovich, Petr Vaclavek, Ron Dale

Printed in the United States of America in
Stevens Point, Wisconsin
092014   008479WZS15

TABLE OF CONTENTS

IT LOOKS REAL!

Special effects make vampires and aliens look lifelike in movies. Actors bleed, monsters walk, and people grow old in movies. How do makeup artists create these special effects?

special effect—a misleading image created for movies by using makeup, special props, camera systems, computer graphics, and other methods

FAKE TEETH

Makeup artists create fake teeth and vampire fangs. Artists also make crooked teeth, extra teeth, and sharp teeth. They may even make it look like actors have missing teeth.

Makeup artists make **molds** of an actor's teeth. Then artists add crooked or pointed tooth shapes to the molds. Last, plastic copies of the creepy new teeth are made. The fake plastic teeth fit over an actor's real teeth.

mold—a model of an object

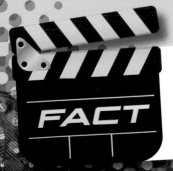

FACT

Yellow, brown, and red paints make teeth appear missing or damaged.

CREATING WOUNDS

Actors pretend to get hurt during fights, car crashes, and falls. Artists make fake wounds using **derma wax**. They add small pieces of the wax to actors' bodies. Artists then shape and color the wax to look like wounds.

derma wax—see-through wax that is easy to shape and sticks well to skin

11

Makeup artists also use wax to create more serious injuries. They split the wax with a **spatula** to make it look like the actor was cut. The artist dabs brown and red makeup on the wax. The coloring makes the cut look real.

spatula—a sculpting tool with a flat, rounded, bendable blade

MAKING ACTORS BLEED

Makeup artists use corn syrup and food coloring to make fake blood. To make the blood squirt from wounds, artists put tubes of fake blood under **foam latex** makeup. They use a **remote control** to make the tubes burst.

foam latex—a soft, lightweight, spongy material

remote control—a device used to make things happen from a distance

FACT

Director Alfred Hitchcock used chocolate syrup for fake blood in his black-and-white movies. Movie audiences could not tell the fake blood was not red.

What if a character gets punched in the mouth? An artist puts a small case filled with red powder in an actor's mouth. When the actor bites the case, the powder mixes with spit. Fake blood drips from the actor's mouth.

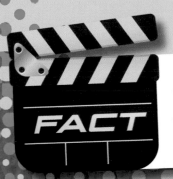

FACT

Fake blood is sometimes flavored with peppermint.

FUNNY FACES

Actors change their faces for movies. Makeup artists use **alginate** to create a mold of an actor's face. The dried mold is filled with **plaster**. Clay warts and alien ears can be added to the dried plaster. The plaster mold is used to make a rubber mask that fits an actor's face.

alginate—a material used to make molds

plaster—a white powder made from a soft rock that creates a paste when mixed with water

GOING BALD

Makeup artists use bald caps to make an actor look bald. Artists wet an actor's hair and then pull the bald cap over the actor's head. An artist cuts the cap to fit and glues the edges to the actor's skin.

A LITTLE HAIRY

Sometimes actors need more hair. Artists make wigs, beards, and moustaches. They use human, animal, or man-made hair. They create wigs and beards by tying hair to **mesh**. They glue the finished pieces to the actor's skin.

mesh—material made of threads that are woven together with spaces in between

FACT Artists sometimes poke single hairs into foam latex makeup. They use hair-punching needles to make hairy werewolf arms.

DEAD BODIES

Sometimes movie characters die. Artists apply pale-colored makeup over the actor's skin. They sometimes **tint** the makeup with blue or yellow. Red-brown makeup dabbed around eyes gives them a sunken look.

tint—to change a color slightly

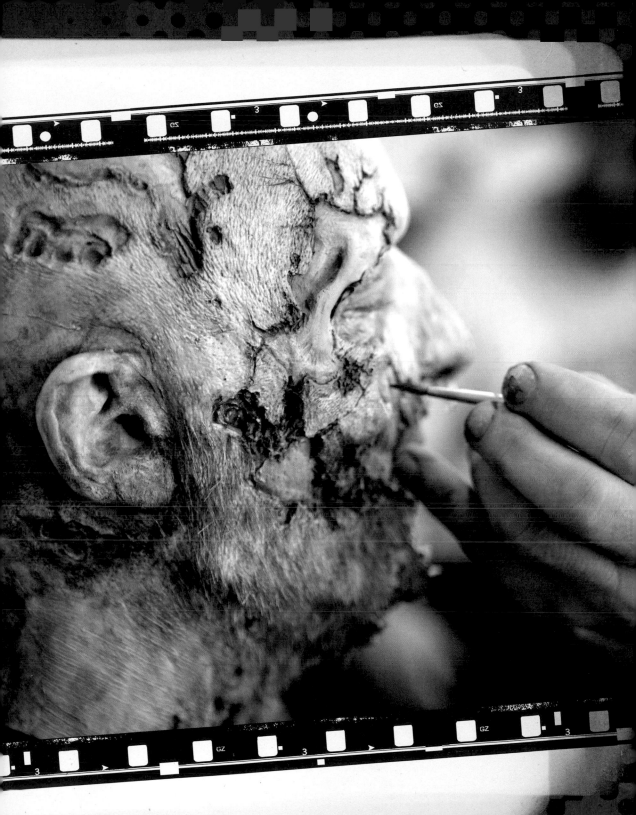

25

AGING ACTORS

Movie magic can make a young actor look old. Artists dab **latex** makeup on an actor's face. Then artists pull the skin on an actor's face up from the cheekbones.

latex—a rubbery material that stretches

Dustin Hoffman aged about 90 years in the 1970 movie *Little Big Man*. Artists glued painted latex on his face (right) and hands to make him look older.

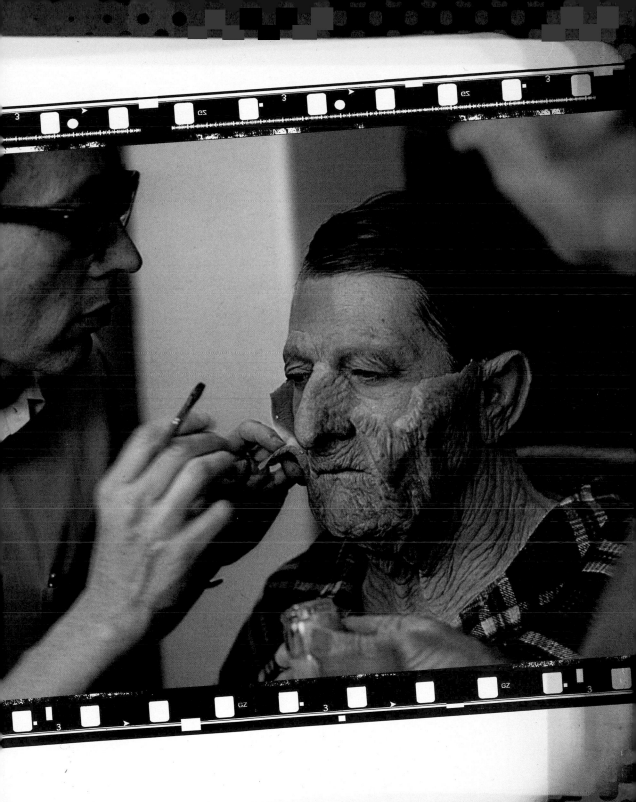

After the latex dries, artists let go of the actor's skin. The dried latex makes the actor's skin seem wrinkled. Special effects makeup artists change actors into amazing characters. The possibilities are nearly endless!

GLOSSARY

alginate (AL-juh-nayt)—a material used to make molds

derma wax (DER-muh WHAX)—see-through wax that is easy to shape and sticks to skin

foam latex (FOHM LAY-tex)—a soft, lightweight, spongy material

latex (LAY-tex)—a rubbery material that stretches

mesh (MESH)—material made of threads that are woven together with spaces in between

mold (MOHLD)—a model of an object

plaster (PLASS-tur)—a white powder made from a soft rock that creates a paste when mixed with water

remote control (ri-MOHT kuhn-TROHL)—a device used to make things happen from a distance

spatula (SPA-choo-luh)—a sculpting tool with a flat, rounded, bendable blade

special effect (SPESH-uhl uh-FEKT)—a misleading image created for movies by using makeup, special props, camera systems, computer graphics, and other methods

tint (TINT)—to change a color slightly

READ MORE

Colson, Mary. *Being a Makeup Artist.* Awesome Jobs. Minneapolis: Lerner Publications Company, 2013.

Craig, Jonathan. *Special Effects Make-up Artist.* The Coolest Jobs on the Planet. Chicago: Capstone Raintree, 2014.

Miles, Liz. *Movie Special Effects.* Culture in Action. Chicago: Raintree, 2010.

INTERNET SITES

FactHound offers a safe, fun way to find Internet sites related to this book. All of the sites on FactHound have been researched by our staff.

Here's all you do:

Visit *www.facthound.com*

Type in this code: 9781491420027

Check out projects, games and lots more at
www.capstonekids.com

INDEX